17310

Famous

DRUM SOLOS
AND FILLS

Ted
Reed

FOREWORD

If you found book No. 1, "Drum Solos and Fill-ins", interesting, you will find this book even more challenging, interesting and useful.

The solos and fills contained in this book were inspired by one of the greatest drummers in the world. He is world known for his flawless technique, speed, great drum solos and fills.

It is hoped that this book will inspire and help you to play your own solos and fills.

You will find that these solos will also sound good if played a little slower than the tempo indicated.

CODE

Cymbal   Strike the ride cymbal with the tip of the stick.

S.T.T.   Small tom-tom.

S.D.   Snare drum.

L.T.T.   Large tom-tom.

B.D.   Bass drum.

RS   Rim shot.

R on L Right on left stick shot.

Buzz
roll

Buzz each stick simultaneously in the form of an open "V".

R
L

Play the hi hat on two and four.

After you have mastered each solo, precede and follow it with four bars of basic rhythm, as follows;

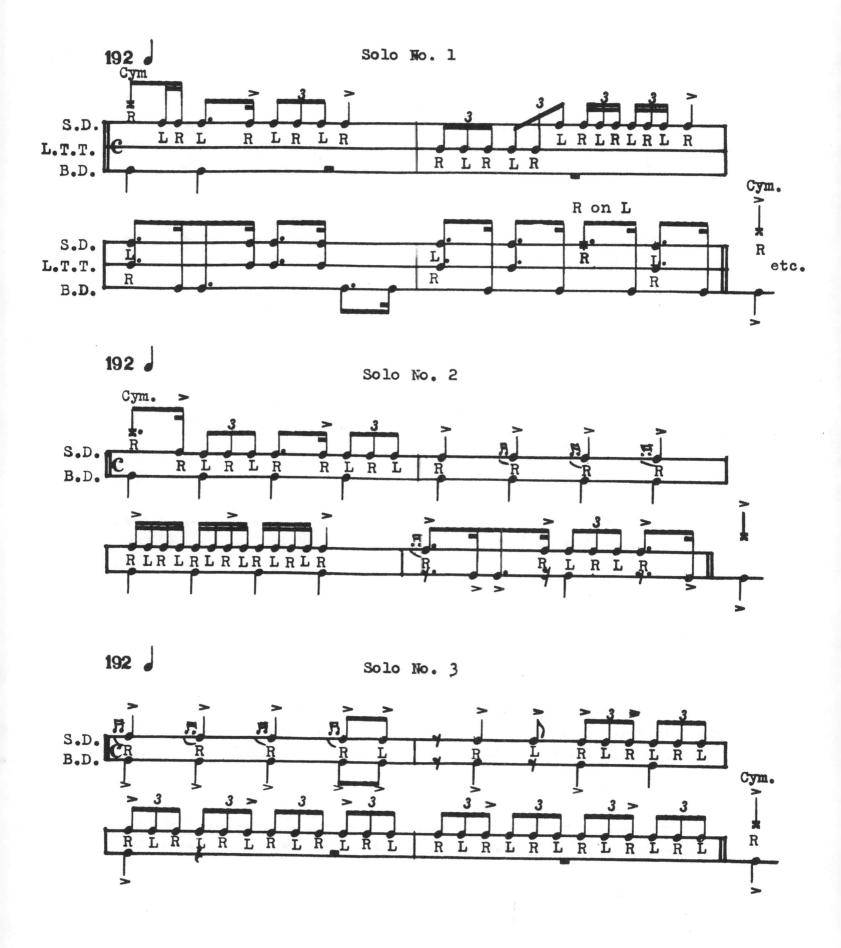

Solo No. 1

Solo No. 2

Solo No. 3

4

Solo No. 4

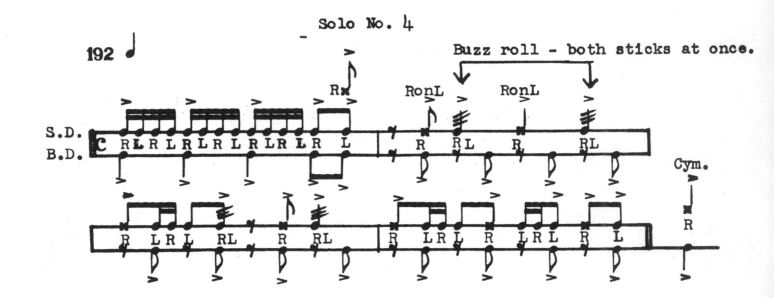

Solo No. 5

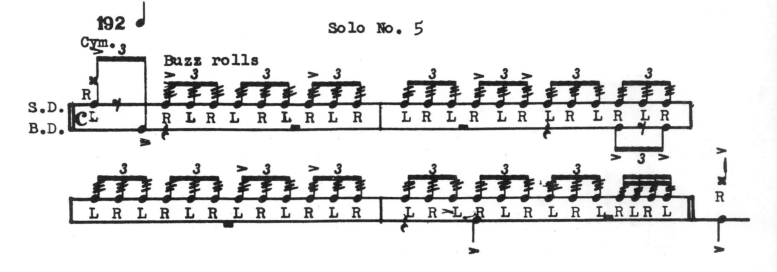

Solo No. 6

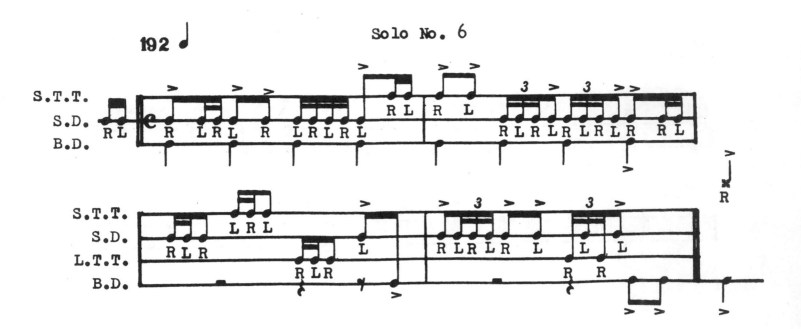

Solo No. 7

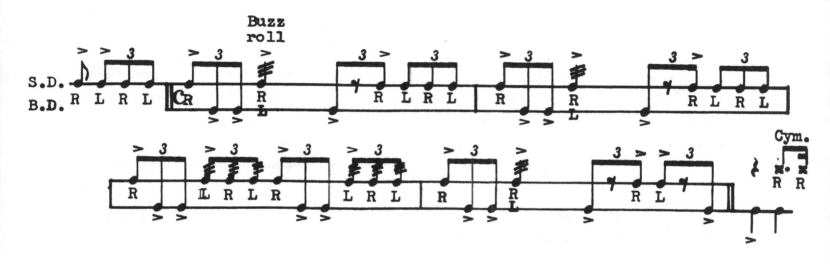

Solo No. 8

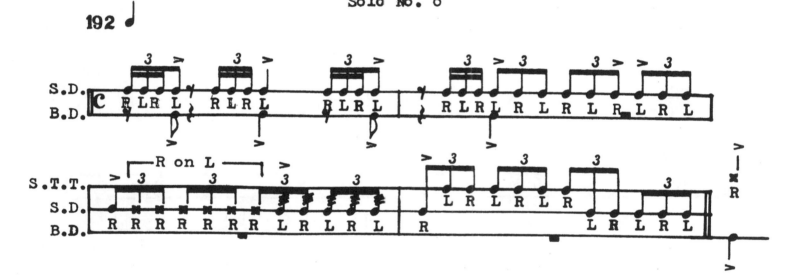

Solo No. 9

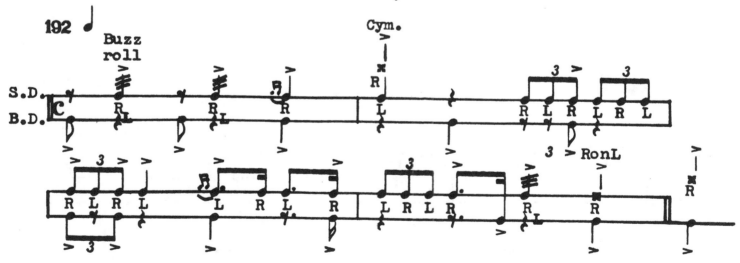

6

Solo No. 10

Solo No. 11

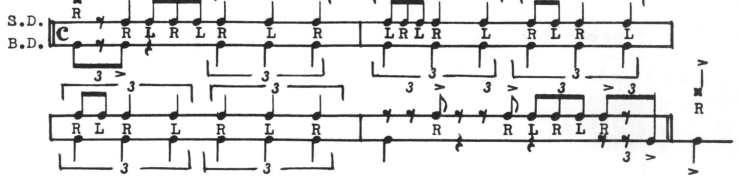

Solo No. 12

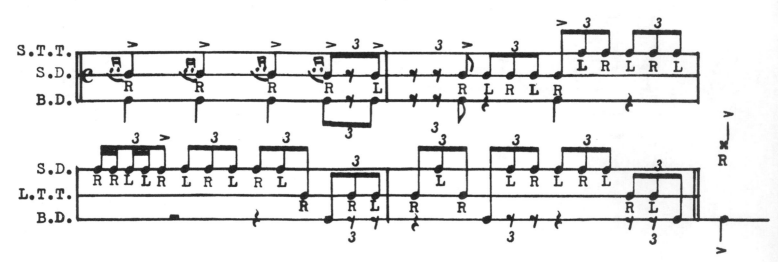

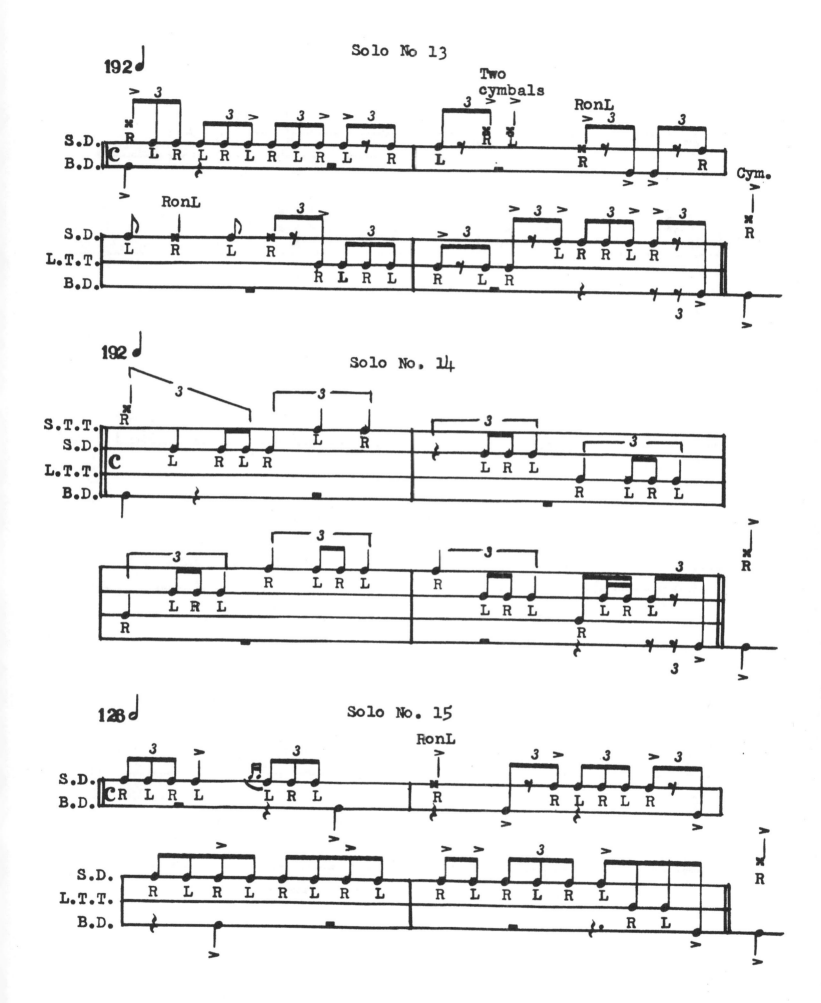

Solo No 13

Solo No. 14

Solo No. 15

8

192 ♩ Solo No. 16

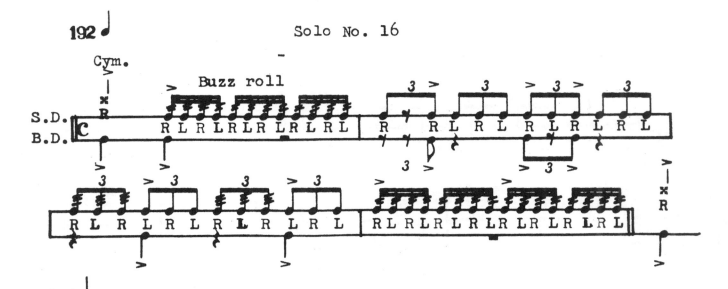

184 ♩ Solo No. 17

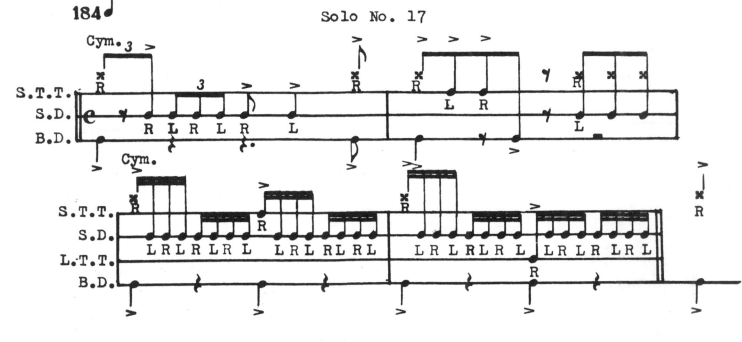

192 ♩ Solo No. 18

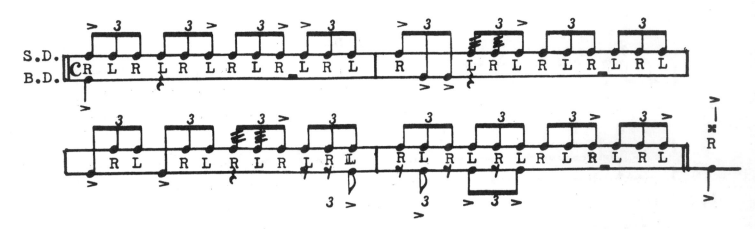

Solo No. 19

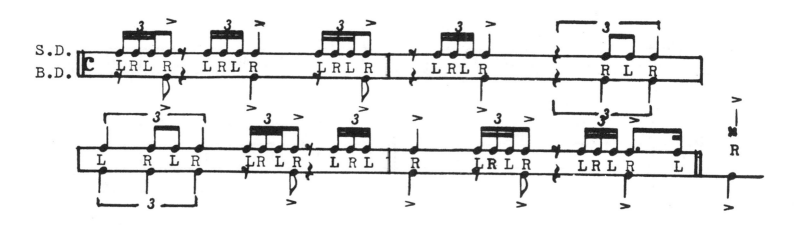

Solo No. 20

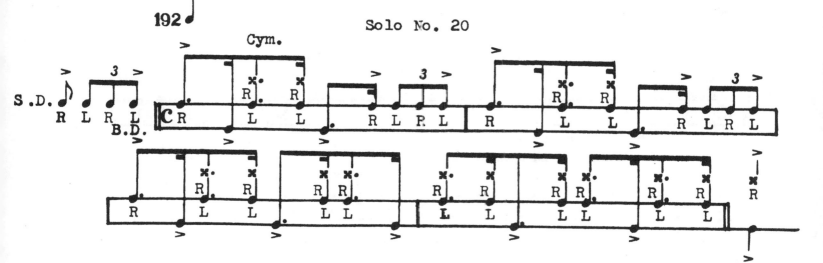

Solo No. 21

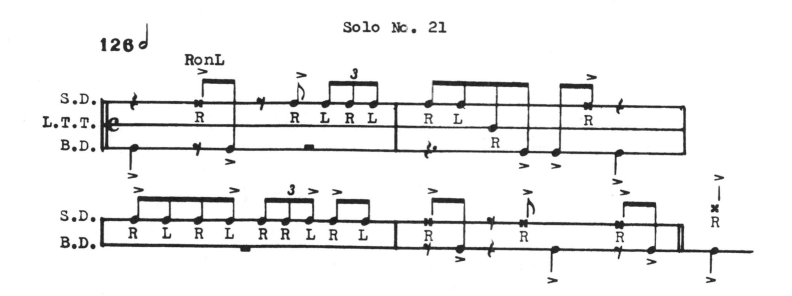

10

Solo No. 22

126 ♩

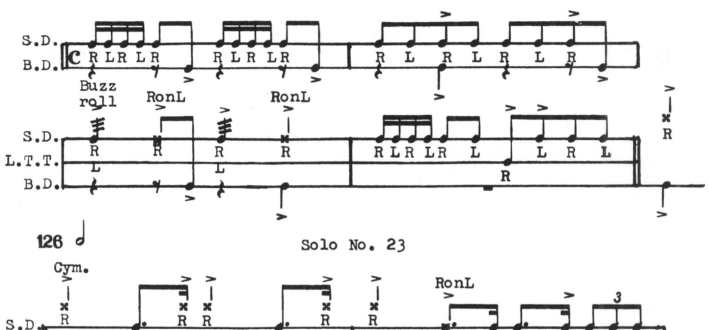

126 ♩

Solo No. 23

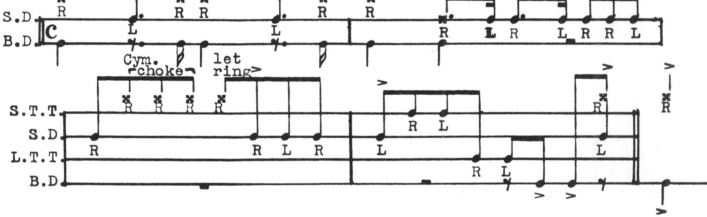

Solo No. 24

138 ♩

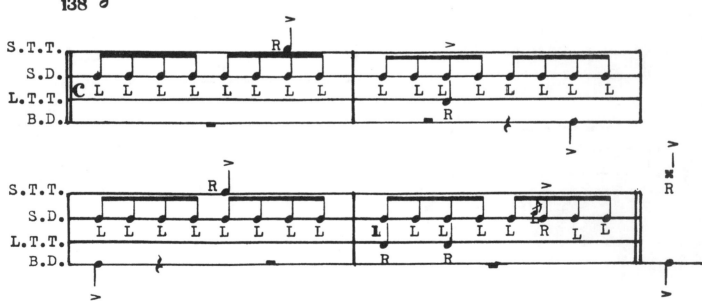

Solo No. 25

160

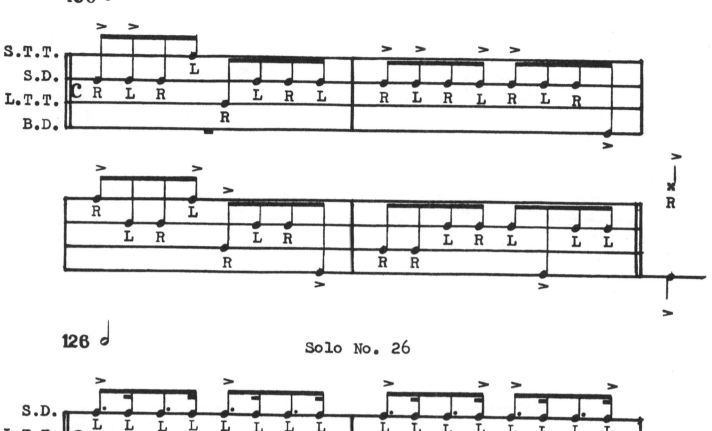

Solo No. 26

126

Solo No. 27

126

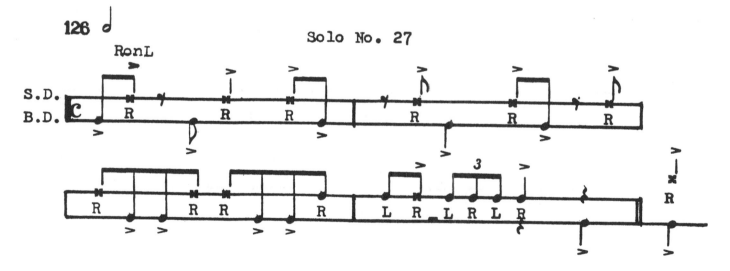

12

Solo No. 28

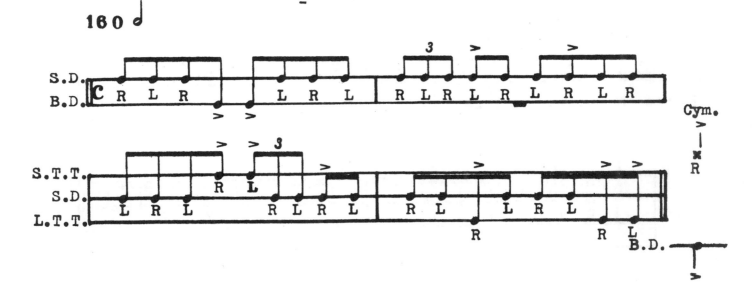

Solo No. 29

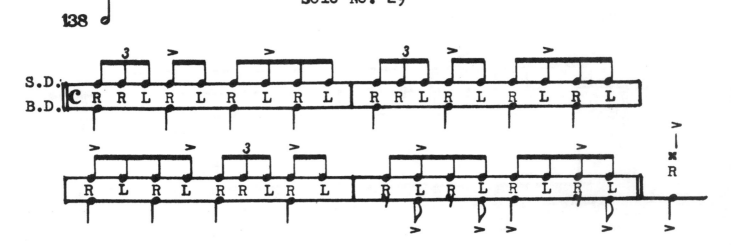

Solo No. 30

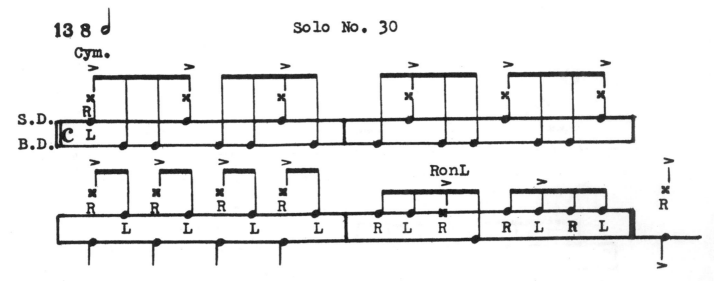

Solo No. 31

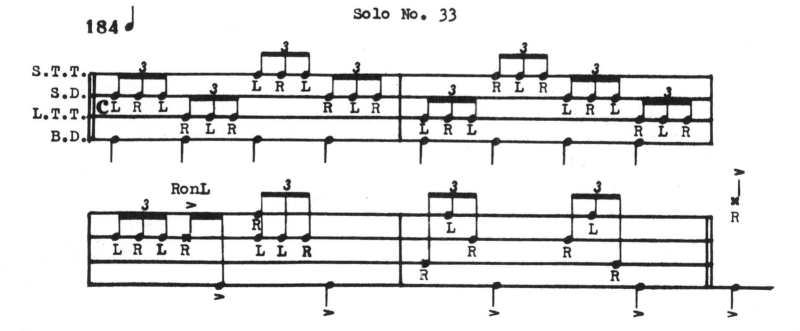

Solo No. 32

Solo No. 33

Solo No. 34

160 ♩

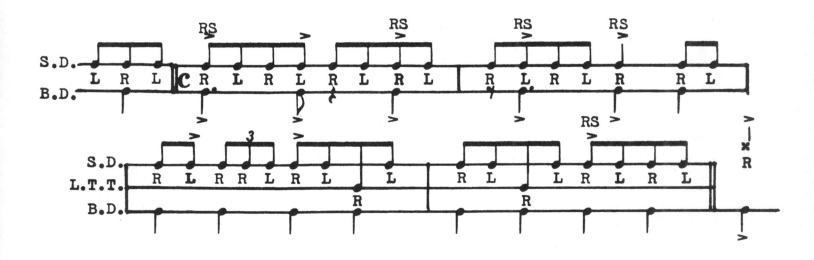

Solo No. 35

160 ♩

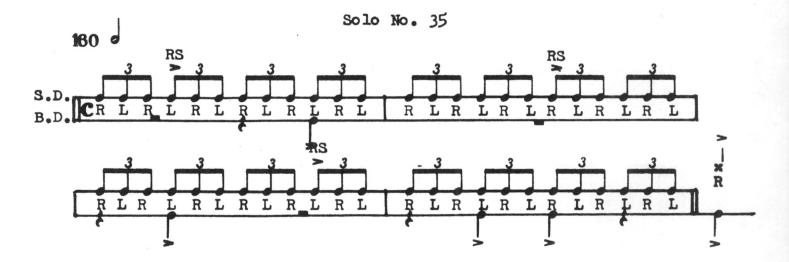

Solo No. 36

200 ♩

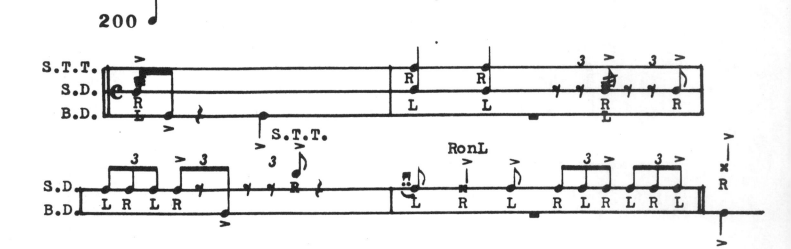

Solo No. 37

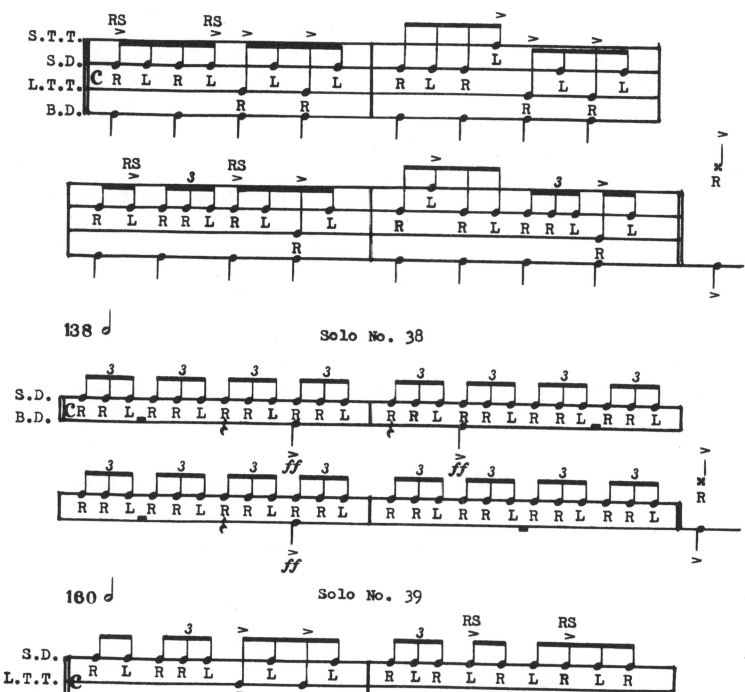

Solo No. 38

Solo No. 39

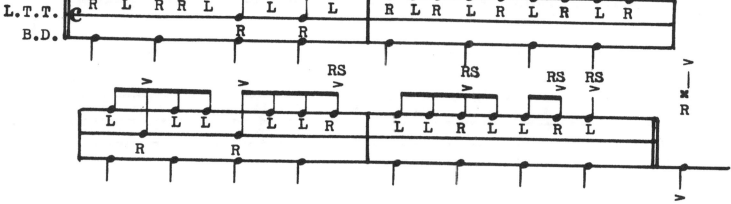

Solo No. 40

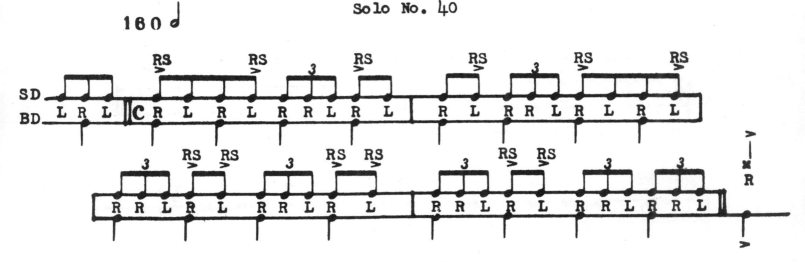

Solo No. 41

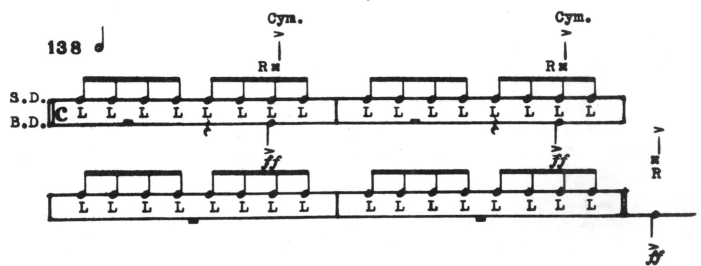

Solo No. 42

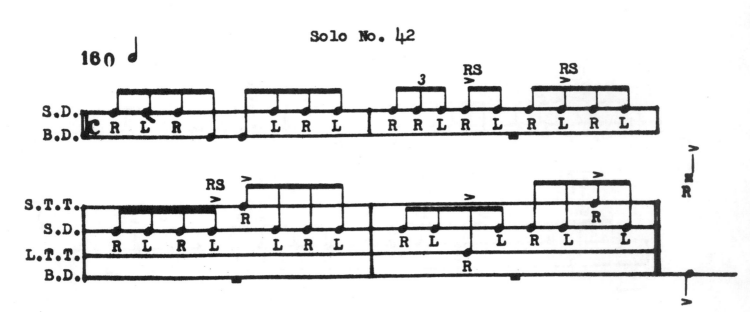

Solo No. 43

160 ♩

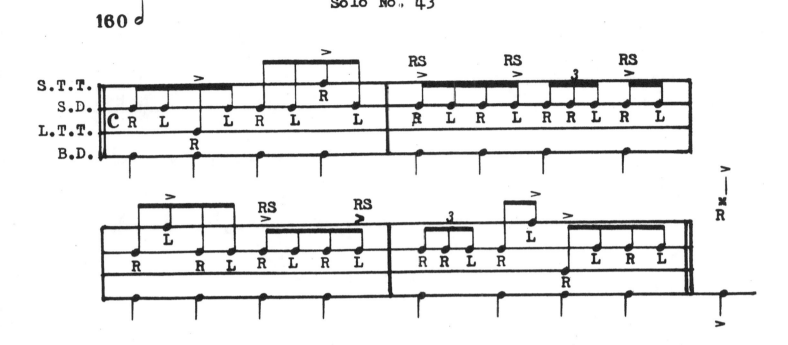

Solo No. 44

160 ♩

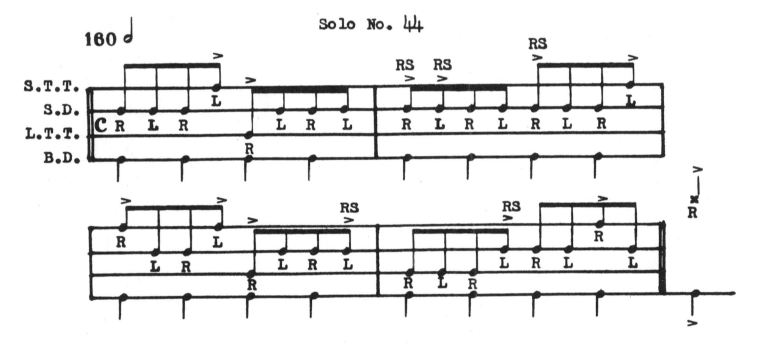

Solo No. 45

138 ♩

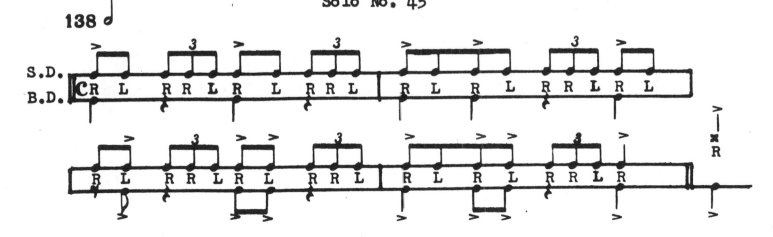

18

Solo No. 46

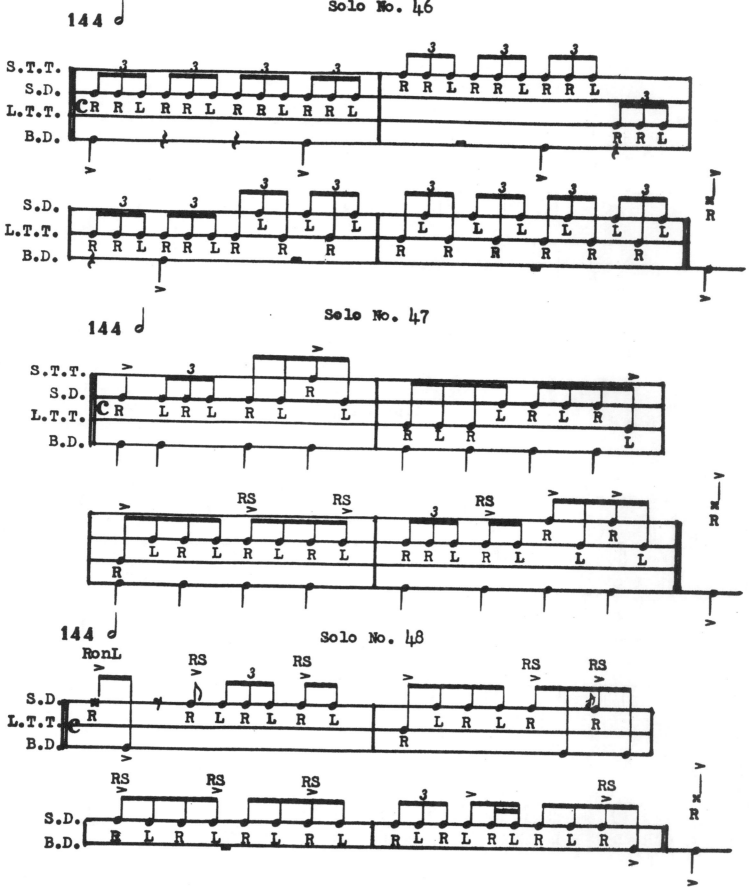

Solo No. 47

Solo No. 48

Solo No.49

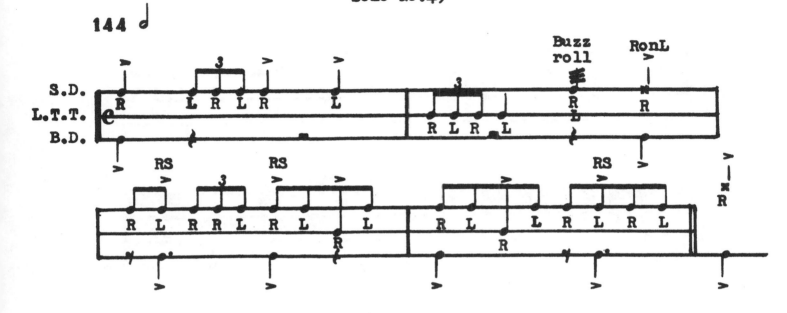

Solo No. 50

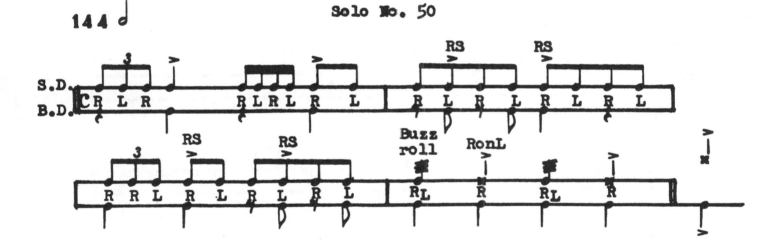

Solo No. 51

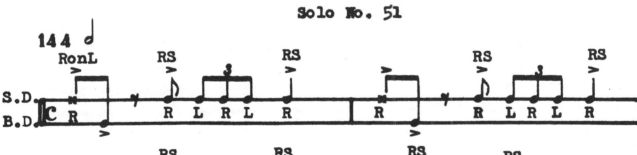

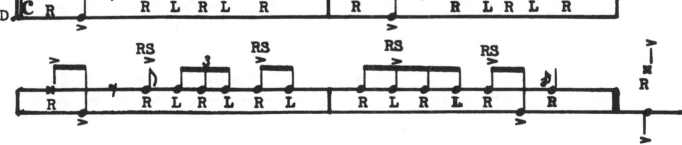

Solo No. 52

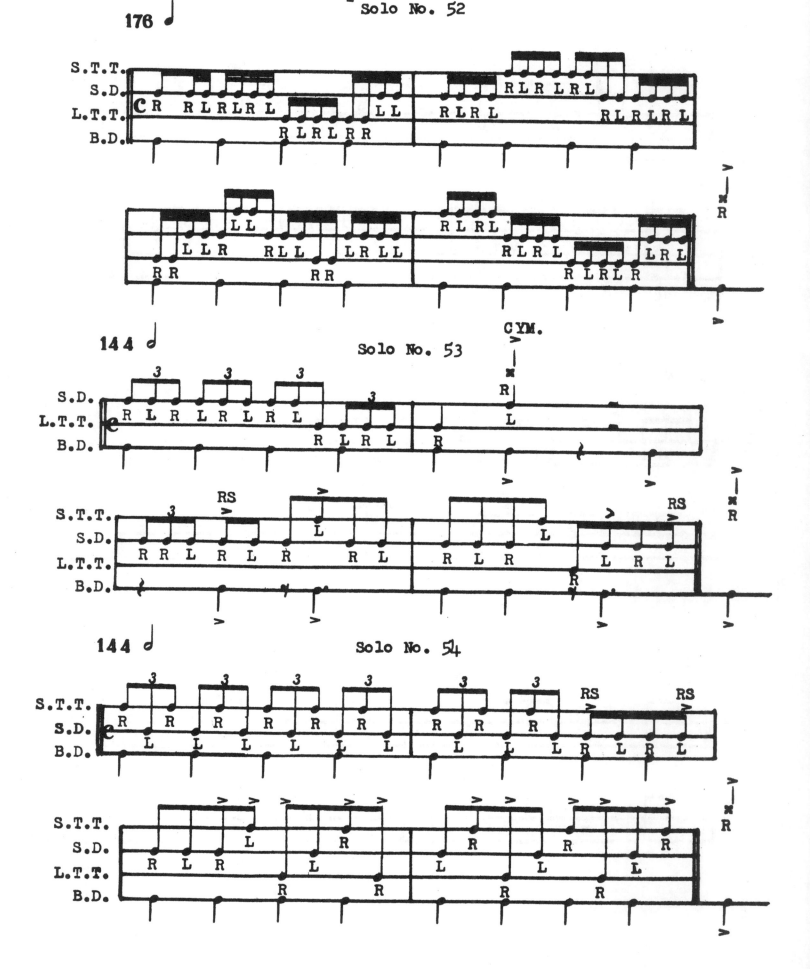

Solo No. 53

Solo No. 54

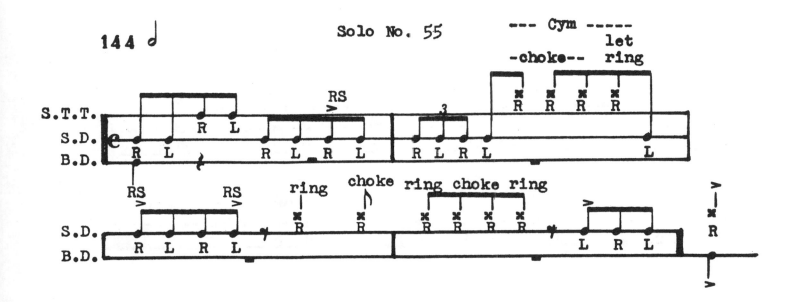

Solo No. 55

Solo No. 56

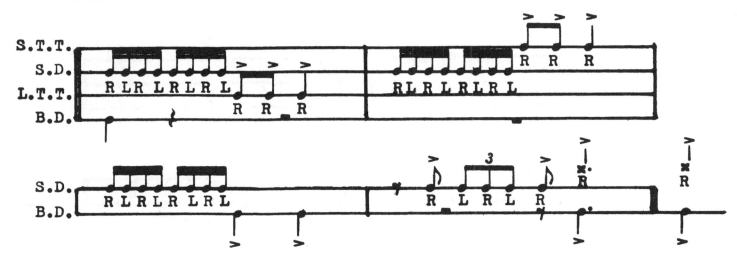

Solo No. 57

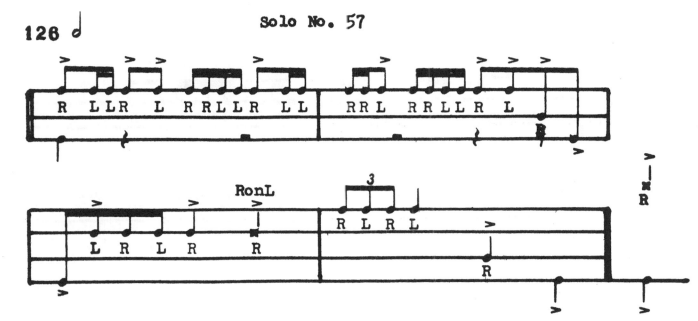

21

Solo No. 58

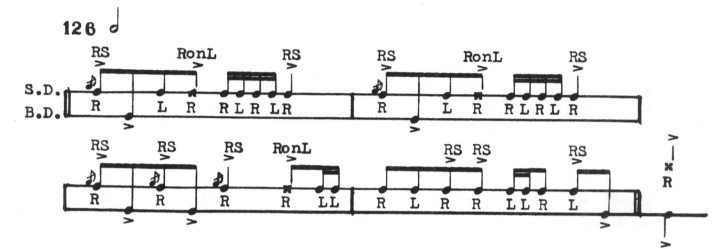

Solo No. 59

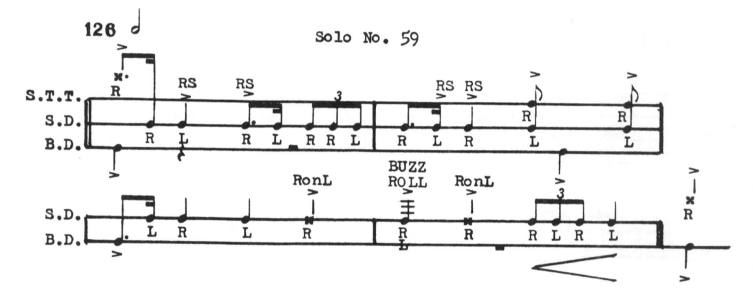

Solo No. 60

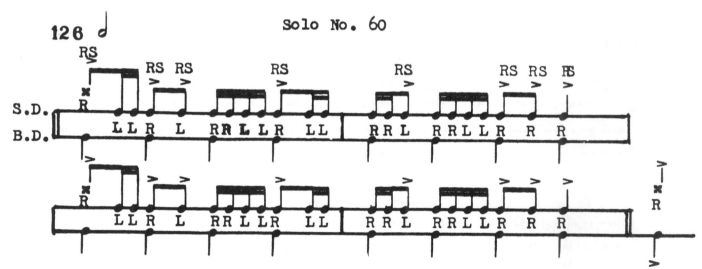

Solo No. 61

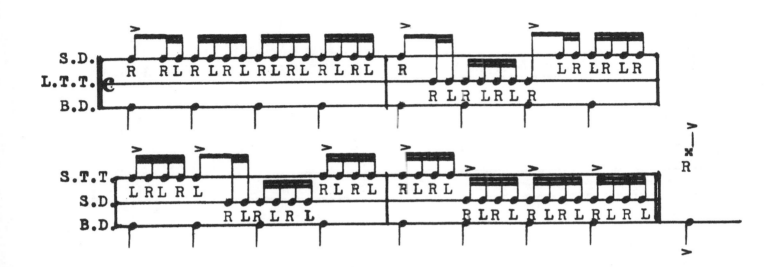

Solo No. 62

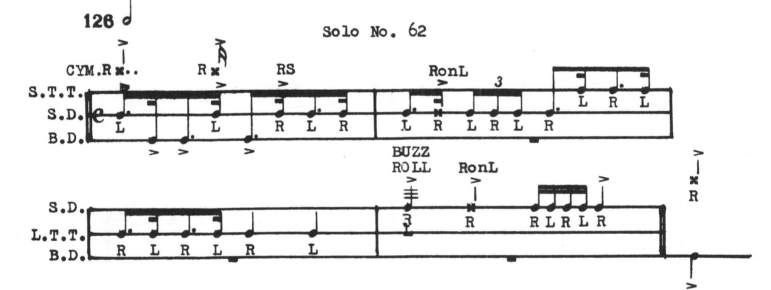

Solo No. 63

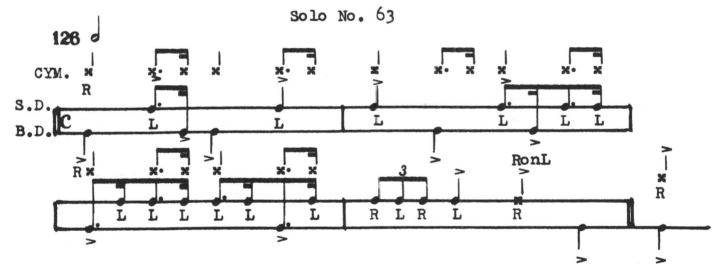

Solo No. 64

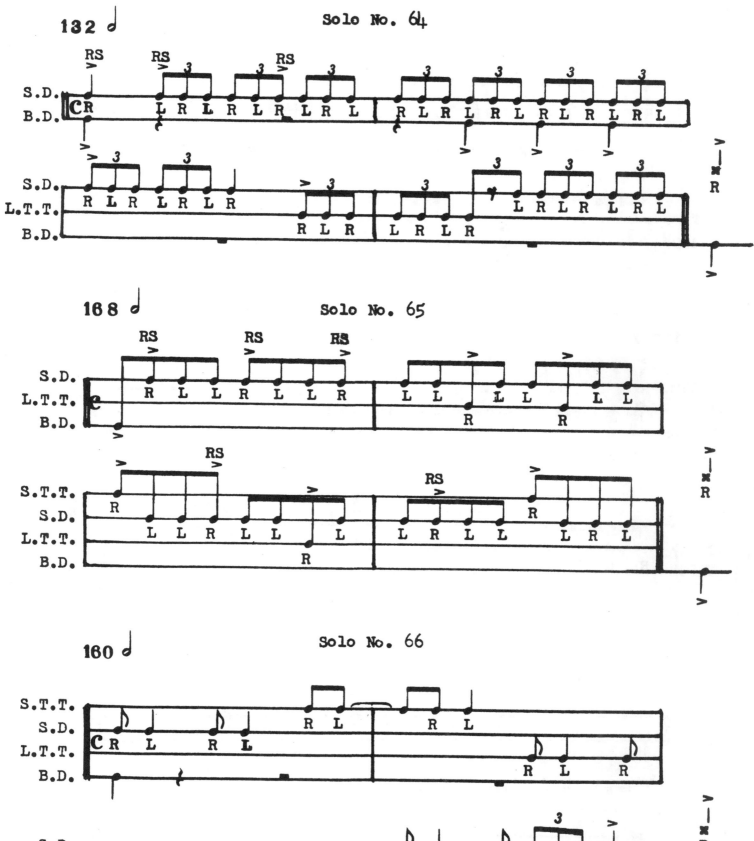

Solo No. 65

Solo No. 66

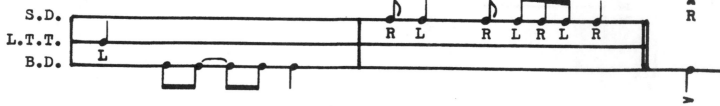

Solo No. 67

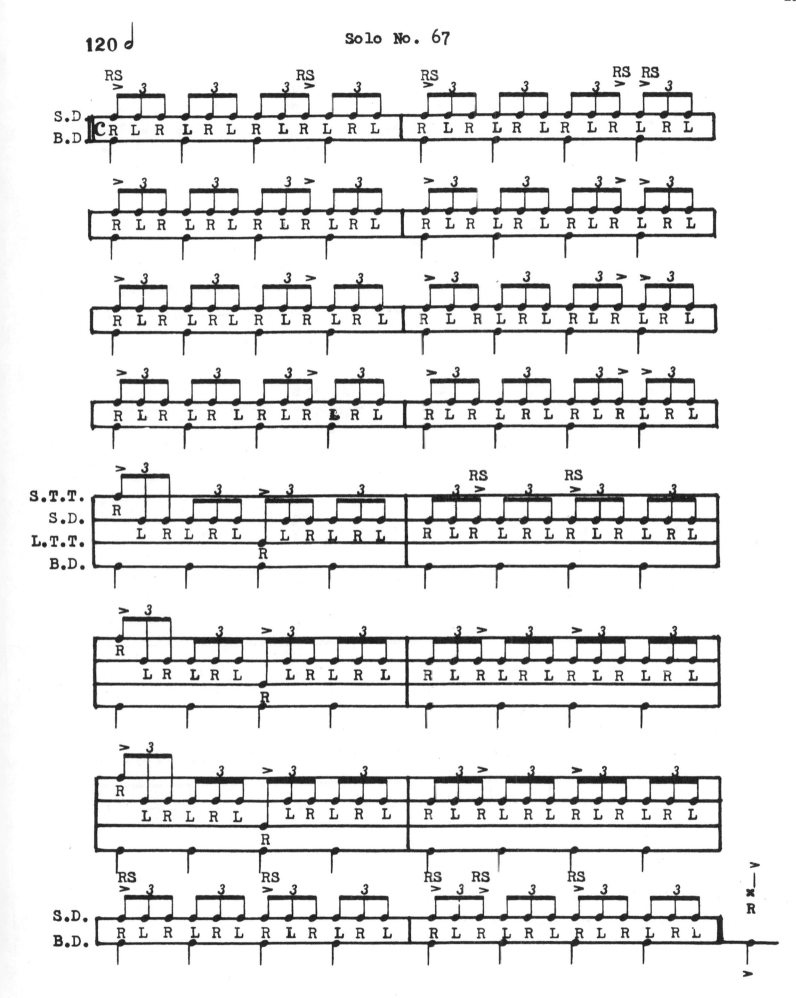

Solo No. 68

Solo No. 69

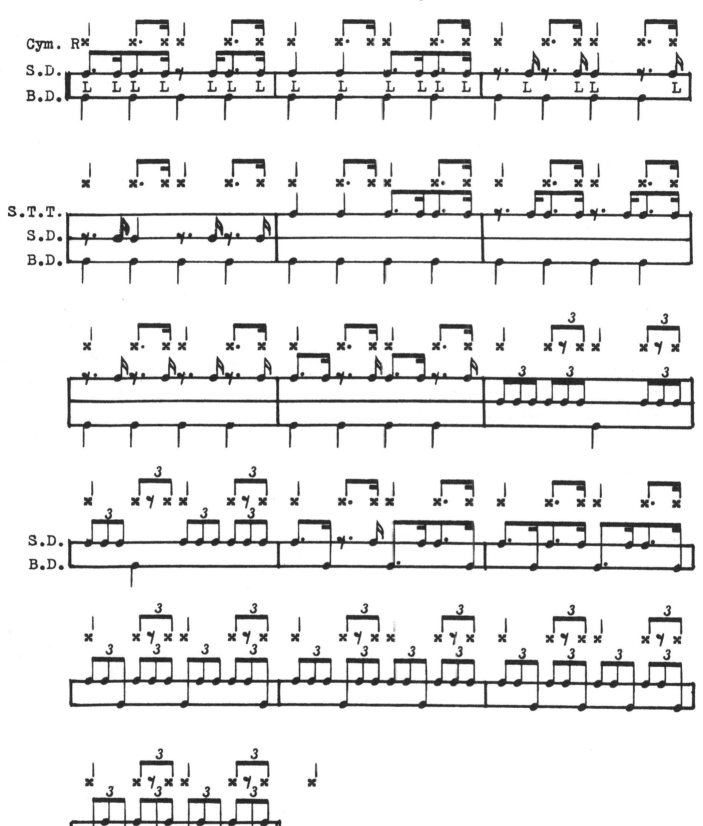

FILL-INS

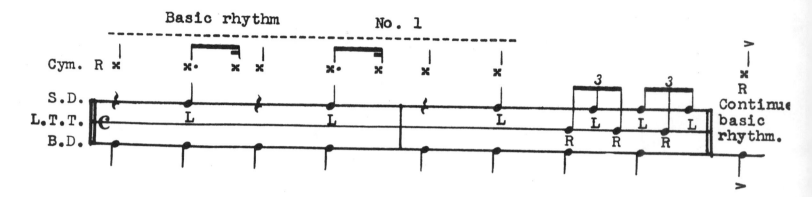

No. 2

No. 3

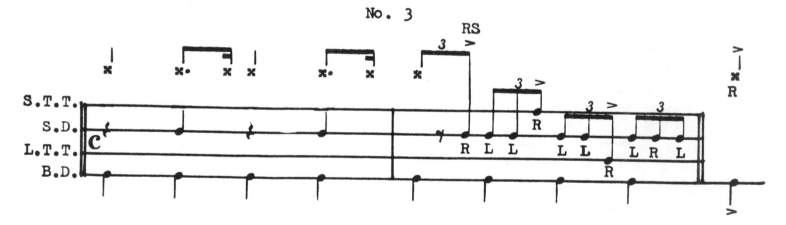

No. 4

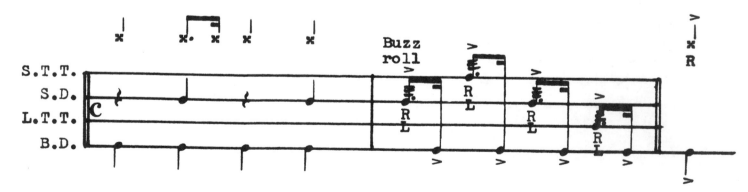

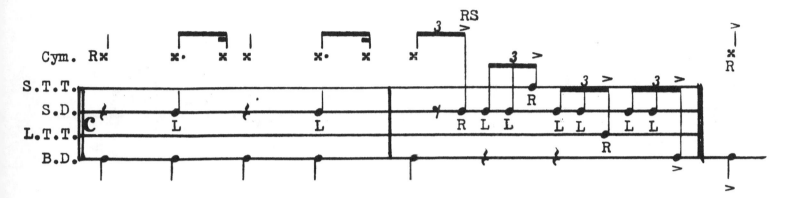

No. 5

No. 6

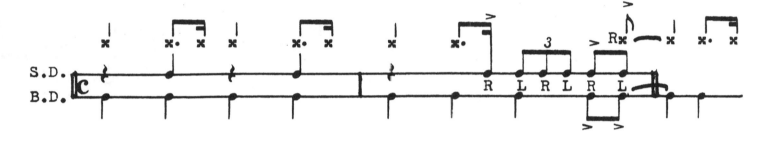

No. 7

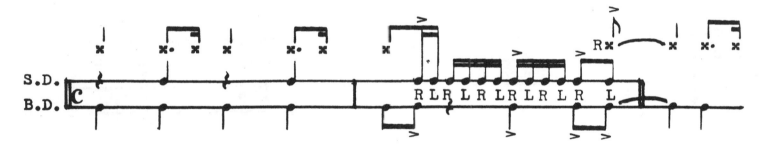

No. 8

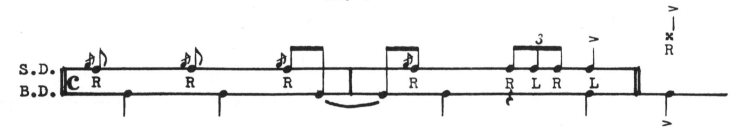

No. 9

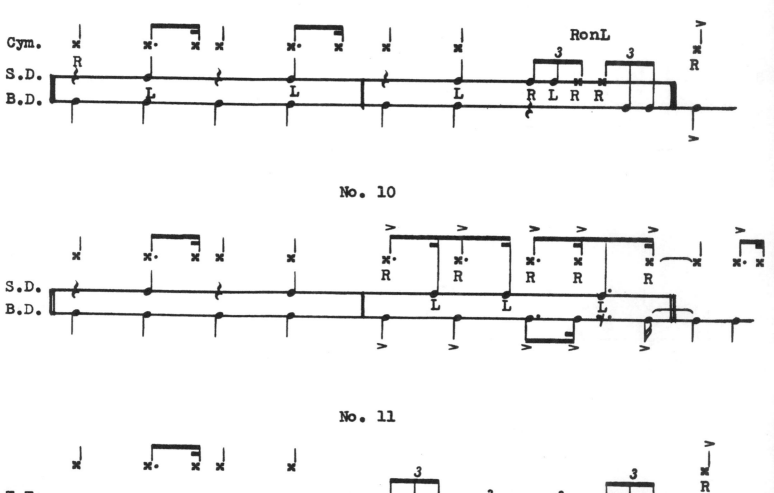

No. 10

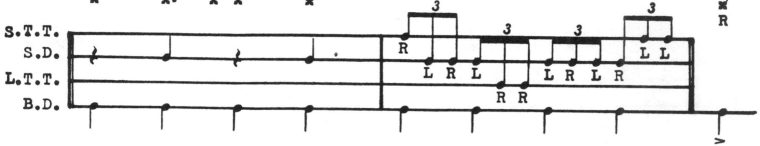

No. 11

No. 12

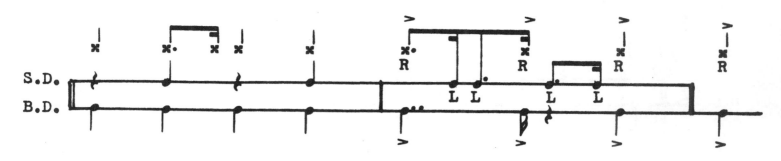

No. 13

No. 14

No. 15

No. 16

No. 17

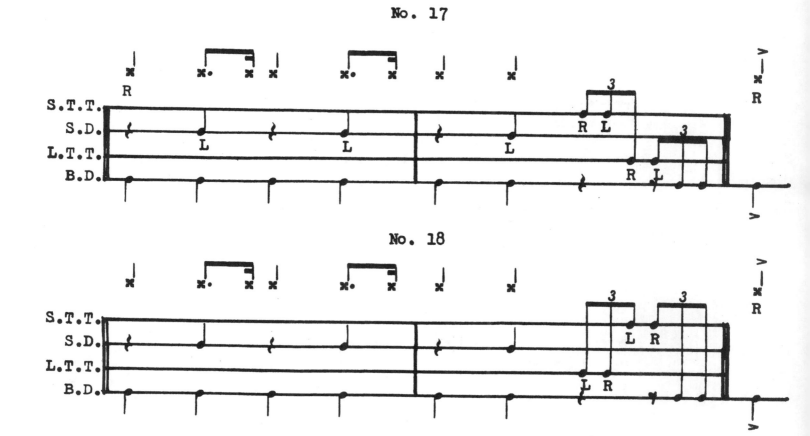

No. 18

No. 19

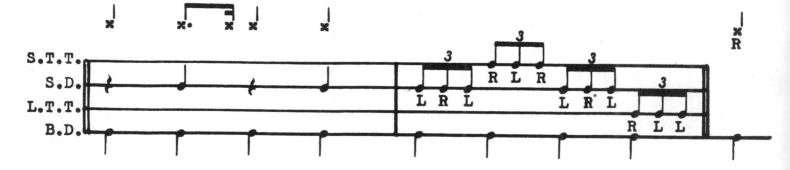

No. 20

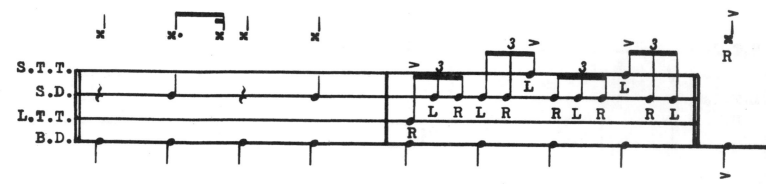